ICONS

YT **DE YTURBE** ARQUITECTOS
MEXICO

TURNER

YT **DE YTURBE** ARQUITECTOS

Editing, Selection and Editorial Coordination
Jimena Gutiérrez • De Yturbe Arquitectos • Frontespizio • Turner México

Graphic Design
Ricardo Salas & Frontespizio 2008

Texts
Alberto Blanco
Igor Moreno

A selection of quotes taken from Alberto Blanco's personal library accompany the various photographs illustrating the architecture of De Yturbe Arquitectos

Photography
© *Alfonso de Béjar*
© *Michael Calderwood*
© *Fernando Cordero*
© *Paul Czitrom*
© *De Yturbe Archive*
© *Miguel García*
© *Luis Gordoa*
© *Mario Mutschlechner*
© *Grupo Posadas*
© *Undine Prohl*
© *Arturo Zavala Haag*

Translation
Ruiz-Vivanco y Asociados S.C. and Ricardo Piña for *Mexican Architectural Firm, De Yturbe Arquitectos* by Igor Moreno
Suzanne Stephens for Alberto Blanco and Pedro Salinas
Debra Nagao for José Yturbe's introduction

Copy Editing
Debra Nagao

Production
Turner México

First edition, 2008
D.R. © De Yturbe Arquitectos, S.A. de C.V.
Monte Cáucaso, Lomas de Chapultepec, México, D.F. 11000

First edition, 2008
D.R. © Editorial Turner de México, S.A. de C.V.
Anatole France 13, Chapultepec Polanco, México, D.F. 11560
Tel. 52 82 33 64
ISBN 978-968-9056-41-6

Made in Mexico • *Printed in Spain*

Distribuited in Mexico and Latin America through
Editorial Océano de México S.A. de C.V.
Blvd. Manuel Ávila Camacho No. 76 Piso 10
Colonia Lomas de Chapultepec, C.P. 11000, México D.F.
www.oceano.com.mx

Distribuited in Europe through
Turner Publicaciones
C/ Rafael Calvo, 42-2° esc.izda, 28010 Madrid
www.turnerlibros.com

Idea Books
Nieuwe Herengracht 11, Ámsterdam 1011 RD, Holanda
www.ideabooks.nl

Art Data
12 Bell Industrial Estate, 50 Cunnington Street, London W4 5HB
www.artdata.co.uk

Distribuited in the United States through
D.A.P. Distributed Art Publishers
155 Sixth Avenue, 2nd Floor, New York, NY 10013
www.artbook.com

CONTENTS

INTRODUCTION

José de Yturbe

I BEGAN THIS ADVENTURE IN 1966 BY DESIGNING MY PARENTS' HOME in Valle de Bravo. Working alone and at night, I would show them whenever I had something ready. The three us of would look it over, as if it were a secret plan. The ideas matured until one day we decided the project was ready.

Tito Beraud, a well-known figure in Valle de Bravo, built it. The project had an 11-meter free-span in the living room. Tito managed to get a huge 13-meter beam from the forest, floating it across the lake, dragging it to the building site, raising it and putting it in place.

Today this beam continues to sustain the house, despite the opinion of a number of distinguished architects from the time who said it would never hold up. Once the doubt was raised, I asked the head worker his opinion and with the characteristic certainty of years of experience, he assured me that yes, it would stand!

With time, my list of clients began to grow . . .

Today my firm is no longer mine alone; it belongs to many others. DE YTURBE ARQUITECTOS is sustained, like the beam, by my son José, by Andrés Cajiga, and many individuals who have collaborated and continue to collaborate with us. Thanks to all of them, we are working in such faraway and complex places as Europe, the Arabian Peninsula, India, Mexico, and Central America, and one day we hope to reach China and Russia.

I am indebted to a number of architects, starting with Luis Barragán. Although I never worked with him, I learned by visiting his buildings and his house. His lessons included a taste

for beauty, the importance of space, the path of movement, light, the element of surprise, and the placement of furnishings.

I am grateful to Juan Sordo Madaleno, with whom I have worked in several stages of my life. For example, during his years as an architect and a promoter, I would like to express my thanks for supporting me in hard times, with his characteristic intelligence and generosity.

I would also like to thank Augusto H. Álvarez, Enrique de la Mora y Palomar, Andrés Casillas, and Luigi W. Moretti in Rome. By receiving me in their studios, they have transmitted to me the trade of Architecture.

And finally, I would like to express my gratitude to Juan Sordo Madaleno's daughter, Malena, my wife, who knows the trade more than anyone else, for it is in her blood, and just as I have learned from all my mentors, I have learned and continue to learn from her. I thank her for her generosity, her ongoing support, and her confidence in me.

JOSÉ DE YTURBE BERNAL

THE ICONS
OF JOSÉ DE YTURBE

ALBERTO BLANCO

'ICON' IS A WORD THAT COMES FROM THE FRENCH *icône*, WHICH comes from the Russian *ikona*, which in turn is derived from Byzantine Greek. The Greek word *eikon* means image, without implying or saying anything about the holiness or worship of the image.

However, according to the etymological dictionary, an icon is:

1

A religious representation, whether painted or in relief, used in oriental Christian churches.

2

A panel painted using the Byzantine technique.

3

A sign that resembles the object represented such as the signs indicating a crossroads, road works or bend in the highway.

4

A schematic graphic representation used to identify functions or programs.

In other words: an icon is a religious representation; a work of art; a sign or a graphic representation.

In short, combining them all into a single, two-fold definition: an icon is a work of art representing a religious aspiration, or simply a sign denoting a particular function.

FOREWORD

*Art
in a broad sense,
is the form of life
or the sound or color of life.
Regarded as a form (in the abstract)
it is often indistinguishable from life itself*

WALLACE STEVENS, "ADAGIA"

ALBERTO BLANCO

LET'S START FROM THE BEGINNING: WE ACCEPT THE TWO-FOLD DEFINITION of icon as a work of art representing a religious aspiration or quite simply, a sign denoting a certain function, just as we accept the impulse that led the editors of this book, Ricardo Salas and Jimena Gutiérrez, to entitle it *Icons*.

Describing architecture as an art depicting a religious aspiration or a sign denoting a function is obviously too much of a generalization, but at least it does not betray the spirit of the work. Because, although talking about the religious aspirations of a work of art is a bit of a tautology, the same cannot be said of describing architecture as both a spiritual aspiration and the depiction and full embodiment of an eminently practical function in a work. One thing is quite clear: two different things are involved. One that performs a spiritual function and another that performs a practical function. However, both functions are always combined in the practice of architecture, just as both needs—body and soul—are intimately linked in the lives of all human beings. Because man cannot live by bread alone.

However, what do we mean when we talk about a religious aspiration in architecture? In order to answer that question, I shall refer to two artists: Wallace Stevens and Frank Lloyd Wright, a poet and an architect: if art, as the poet proposes, is broadly speaking, "the shape of life or the sound or color of life," and art is also regarded as a shape (in the abstract) it is often indistinguishable from life itself and if, on the other hand, architecture, as Frank Lloyd Wright would have it, "is life, or at least life itself taking shape and the most sincere document of life as it was also lived, then architecture—as a work of art—represents

15

the religious aspiration of giving life shape; of giving it sound and color and of giving life meaning and of offering the most sincere document possible of life as it has always been lived by us, as human beings, now and always.

However, there is nothing in this definition to tell us what is specific about architecture, or that differentiates it from the other arts. Because architecture, in addition to expressing a spiritual aspiration of lending shape and meaning to life—a desire it shares with all the other arts—and of providing the sincerest possible testimony of life, is an art of space. And as if that were not enough, it is also construction.

For a fuller definition of architecture, we could use Open Letter from Guadalajara, written in 1985 by the architect Ignacio Díaz Morales and signed by Rafael Urzúa and Luis Barragán, which declares:

Architecture is space; while urban space is as much architecture as interior space.

Architecture creates cities, which should be friendly and protect their inhabitants. Architecture should therefore be adapted to its city.

In its simple form, architecture is entirely rooted in functional conditions, but through levels of values, it can achieve the highest sphere of spiritual existence and the universe of pure art.

Architecture is the harmonious combination of elements which, while producing poetry, delimit the spaces where the spirit rules.

As one can already see from this definition, which is similar to the practice of De Yturbe Arquitectos in general and in particular to the way José de Yturbe, the firm's founder, understands his trade, two essential elements emerge of what we can see and understand as architecture: space and the desire to go beyond merely complying with the pragmatic function of providing shelter. What true architecture seeks is to produce an effect which, according to the Letter, could be defined as "the highest sphere of spiritual existence and the universe of pure art." Or, in the words of José de Yturbe himself: "if a space does not produce emotion, then it is simply construction, rather than architecture."

This idea of architecture as a space that produces an emotion is clearly formulated in the texts of Mathias Goeritz, an artist who, unlike Barragán, theorized about the most varied aspects of artistic work and architecture in particular. This is obvious from these two paragraphs from "Manifesto on Emotional Architecture," published in 1954:

Art in general, and naturally architecture too is a reflection of man's spiritual state in his time. But one has the impression that the modern, individualized, intellectual architect sometimes exaggerates—perhaps because he is no longer in close contact with the community—by wishing to overemphasize the rational part of architecture. The result is that 20th century man feels overwhelmed by so much "functionalism," logic and utility within modern architecture.

imposing works: an enormous painting covered in gold leaf whose tight-lipped severity recalls the presence of icons in the cathedrals mentioned in his Manifesto.

He looks for a solution, but neither outdoor aestheticism, understood as "formalism" nor organic regionalism nor dogmatic Confucianism have squarely faced the problem that man – as either a creator or a receiver – of our time aspires to something more than just an adequate, pretty house. He asks – or one day will have to ask – architecture and its modern means and materials for spiritual elevation; simply put: an emotion, like the one the architecture of the pyramid, the Greek temple, the Romanesque or Gothic cathedral and even the Baroque palace gave him in their day. It is only by receiving true emotions from architecture that man will be able to regard it as art once more.

This is how it is understood and implemented by De Yturbe Arquityectos, whose core partners, José de Yturbe Bernal, his son, José de Yturbe Sordo and Andrés Cajiga Ramírez, together with a long list of collaborators over the years, have made these premises their credo ever since 1971 when the firm was founded. The more than two hundred projects undertaken over the years including houses, buildings, corporations, banks, museums, hotels, cultural centers, golf courses and tourist developments in many countries (Mexico, the United States, India, Spain, Costa Rica, Nicaragua and recently Dubai) – speak of an architecture, rooted in noble Mexican building traditions. They have offered a series of functional solutions satisfying both material needs and what Mathias Goeritz described as "spiritual elevation."

It is no coincidence that José de Yturbe's architectural Firm in Lomas de Chapultepec is embellished with one of Goeritz's

I
ARCHITECTURAL MAPMAKING

ALBERTO BLANCO

THIS FIRST CHAPTER ON THE WORK OF DE YTURBE ARQUITECTOS, attempts to place their work within the richly varied panorama of contemporary Mexican architecture, highlighting what separates engineering from architecture, logic from poetry and function from emotion. Complementary pairs of words that designate the two poles between which 20th century Mexican art—like all the other arts—is suspended.

Modern architecture in Mexico can be said to have begun ten to fifteen years after the Revolution which, for obvious reasons, forced the suspension of virtually all the country's architectural activities. Once the economy began to recover, however, the new conditions of the transition period were soon reflected in the work of architects such as Carlos Obregón Santacilia and José Villagrán shortly afterwards. Initially, they both built works in the neo-colonial style fashionable at the time, but they were subsequently inspired by European avant-garde movements to develop a style that reveled in its own expression, creating a personal language which, beyond the nationalism and geometry characteristic of an Art Déco style that incorporated pre-Hispanic motifs and themes (which I call Aztéco), developed into rationalistic modernism in Mexican architecture.

Any revolution imagines a new form of architecture and in this respect, the Mexican Revolution was no exception. Nor was it exceptional that this new architecture should have been based on a dream of fantastic architecture. The fantastic constructions dreamed of by Mexican architects came from two main sources: the architectural ideals of the European avant-garde, particularly those of Le Corbusier and the Bauhaus; and the recovery—if not invention—of a traditional Mexican architecture which some sought among pre-Hispanic ruins, others among three centuries of colonial life and still others among the popular architecture of Mexican villages.

It fell to the generation born during the first fifteen years of the 20th century to imagine the new urban environment after the revolutionary chaos that shook Mexico. José Villagrán, Juan O'Gorman, Enrique del Moral, Enrique Yáñez, Francisco Serrano, Juan Legarreta, Mario Pani, Augusto H. Álvarez, Juan Sordo Madaleno, Carlos Lazo, Manuel Parra and of course Luis Barragán—who deserves a separate chapter all to himself—established the solid bases of contemporary Mexican architecture. They all share the fact that each, like Le Corbusier, Mies van der Rohe and Frank Lloyd Wright, born in the late 19th century, thought up their own form of modernity. They called for the use of local materials for Mexican architecture and adapted the needs of the country to the demands of an international language.

Of all these architects, José Villagrán stood out because of the influence, not only of his work, but also his teaching, which covered several decades until it reached the generation of José de Yturbe, who studied under him. And just as one can see the influence of Le Corbusier and Gropius in Villagrán's first rationalist works, the same can be said of José de Yturbe's early works.

The first functionalist building in Mexico can be said to have been the Health Farm in Tacuba, built in 1925 by José Villagrán and an enthusiastic group of students, foremost among which was Juan O'Gorman. Who would have said then that the adventure of 20th century Mexican architecture would largely have been reflected in the work of this unusual artist? In the course of his about-face that led from his profession of faith in the advantages of functionalism and the postulates of the Bauhaus when he very young to producing fantastic, organic architecture, Juan O'Gorman summarized the paradigm of Mexican architecture that has oscillated between the so-called "international Style" (a term coined in 1932 by Alfred Barr for the exhibition of the same name on European rationalist architecture staged at the New York Museum of Modern Art) and regional, organic, emotional art.

In his criticism of contemporary Mexican architecture in 1952, O'Gorman defined the roots of these two contrary, complementary extremes on the basis of the famous postulates of Le Corbusier, the "instant grandfather" (as he was dubbed by César Vallejo) of all contemporary modern architects, all the tendencies citing him as their predecessor and the guiding spirit—and veritable icon—of their constructive work:

Le Corbusier's *Towards a New Architecture*, which contains the purist thesis of International Style, contains two contradictory definitions of architecture: 1) "A house is a machine for living in." 2) "Architecture is the magnificently skilful interplay of geometric volumes under the action of light." The first formula places architecture in the field of engineering, while the second implies that architecture is an object of contemplation and

the work of Barragán and later on, the work of De Yturbe Arquitectos. As a result of Chucho Reyes, that born colorist whom he referred to as his "only teacher," Luis Barragán understood architecture as though it were a painting: planes dissolve in space, creating an artistic composition with vibrant colors. José de Yturbe also understood the lesson. When the time came, he took up the banner and with his team of architects, took it to a new level.

that its beauty is derived from geometry, meaning that it is therefore an aesthetic abstraction.

Architecture understood as the trade of building machines for living, which was the trend followed by the Bauhaus and the rationalist influence of Mies van der Rohe made itself strongly felt in Mexico and in many of its finest architects during the first half of the 20th century. It was not until Luis Barragán was awarded the prestigious Pritzker Prize in 1982 that the second option pointed out by Le Corbusier—of architecture as the skillful interplay of geometric volumes in relation to light—became the accepted route in Mexico.

Juan O'Gorman, as well as Mathías Goeritz and particularly Luis Barragán, inclined towards an architecture based on imagination, emotion and the recreation of the country's own artistic values and they became forerunners that left their mark on Teodoro González de León, Abraham Zabludovsky, Ricardo Legorreta, Agustín Hernández, Francisco Serrano, Carlos Mijares, Andrés Casillas and the young architects of the next generation: Fernando González Gortázar, Diego Villaseñor, López Baz y Calleja and José de Yturbe himself. His unmistakable stamp can be seen in varying degrees and in many ways in the work of all these architects.

In the case of José de Yturbe, in addition to the undisputed icons of his architectural work, Luis Barragán and Mathias Goeritz, one should also mention Jesús Reyes Ferreira. "He had a wonderful eye," recalls José, "because he taught you how to see." Without this exceptional artist, it would be impossible to understand

II
THE TWO FACES OF JANUS

ALBERTO BLANCO

THE ASSIMILATION OF WORKS OF EUROPEAN MODERNISM INTO Mexican architecture in the late 1920s and 1930s and the development of a modern architecture with its own roots over the following decades constituted the setting for José de Yturbe's years of learning.

The two faces of Janus of Mexican architecture found their finest exponent in the person and work of Luis Barragán. Embodying the resistance to the European cultural hegemony that emerged throughout Latin America, Barragán developed a highly personal form of architecture characterized by simple, imposing forms, large walls with small openings, striking colors, rich textures and traditional materials.

Faced with the apparent dichotomy of an international architecture dominated by technology and functionality and an architecture characteristic of Mexican landscape and traditions, Barragán, while emphasizing the latter, never turned his back on the former. Instead, he drew inspiration from it. After all, there are no new creations that are not based on preceding traditions, just as there are no living traditions that do not require new creations to remain healthy and continue being viable. As Carlos Fuentes so aptly notes in his essay "Luis Barragán y la mirada contigua":

The root of the word "tradition" means to free – *tradere* – in other words, to hand over, to pass from one to another, to free in order to liberate. It is a generous word, meaning hands over, frees and liberates. And while only the most obtuse minds require absolute originality (in other words, *ex nihilo*, out of nothing), freeing an artist's tradition means liberating, exalting and enriching the value of his creativity and that of his predecessors.

I find nothing superfluous in this paragraph by Fuentes. And paraphrasing his words, we could say that as part of the same traditional vocation, the work of De Yturbe Arquitectos hands over, frees and liberates. Without ever aspiring to absolute originality, this team of architects openly acknowledges its debt to its illustrious predecessors. At the same time, they honor this legacy, liberating it and exalting it in the exercise of their own creativity.

Among the sources of inspiration — or, if you will: among the many elective affinities — of José de Yturbe, beyond Barragán's example and the learning, and practical, close relationship with the person who would subsequently become his associate, Juan Sordo Madaleno, with whom he worked at a very early stage at the María Isabel Hotel and the architects Augusto H. Álvarez, De la Mora and Andrés Casillas and Italian architect Luigi Moretti, with whom he worked for a year in Rome, it is essential to mention the four pillars of 20th century architecture: Le Corbusier, Mies van der Rohe, Gropius and Frank Lloyd Wright.

According to the architectural conception drawn from the work and teachings of Frank Lloyd Wright, a human being's dwelling should be the "vehicle of harmony between man and the earth." However, the architect's idea that "form follows function" was regarded by the new generation as a misunderstanding. Form and function should be a single item, linked in a spiritual sense. The union of form and function in a single work implies that the construction is born, grows, behaves, multiplies and dies, like nature: in an organic way.

The idea of an architecture that goes beyond formalism, functionalism, organic regionalism and academic dogmatism is not new. On the contrary, it is firmly rooted in the traditional art characteristic of traditional societies. This is how Juan O'Gorman eventually understood it when he argued, complementing Frank Lloyd Wright's proposal, that "organic architecture implies the relationship between the building and the surrounding landscape." According to this architectural conception, a human being's dwelling becomes the "vehicle of harmony between man and the earth."

José de Yturbe and his entire team of architects believe in this age-old desire of architecture as a medium that relates the building to the surroundings, which is why he supports the urgent task of protecting the environment and attempts to reverse — as far as possible — the damage caused by our civilization. At the same time, it serves as a vehicle that first of all enables human beings to solve their basic needs of shelter and protection so that it can then set about the task of serving as an instrument that will enable them to adjust their perceptions.

De Yturbe Arquitectos is a firm that has discovered through experience all the necessary elements for turning its work into an instrument that will enable it to capture the spirit of the era and propose perceptions that are in tune with the times. This twofold musical metaphor is merely an echo of the dichotomy that

about architecture: matter and spirit; construction and art; functionalism and emotion? In the words of Luis Barragán: "There are two worlds: One of them exists without people ever talking about them: It is called the real world, because you do not have to talk about it to see it. The other is the world of art, which you have to talk about, because otherwise it would not exist."

endlessly branches out in architecture and all the other arts and which we can see expressed everywhere as a new gesture. on the uncertain threshold of this new millennium, there is a sort of fall towards the elementary and "primitive," a giving in to the simple and minimalist in the face of the relentless advance of science and the predominance of technology.

However, the profound need to reconcile these contradictory, opposing impulses is still there . . . here. And architecture vouches for this need. But it not only vouches for it, but in making its declaration of faith, it tries to turn opposites into complements. This is exactly what is achieved by the constructions of De Yturbe Arquitectos where the modern possibilities of technology in construction seem to be effortlessly combined with the timeless need for peace and quiet in the intimacy of the cave.

These two distinct worlds—one ancestral, the other strictly contemporary—coexist in each of his works. This can be seen on the cover of this book, a veritable icon representing the work of De Yturbe Arquitectos as a team: With a thought-provoking photograph by Miguel García of the "House of Palms" built in 2002 in Punta Mita, Nayarit, showing many of the features characterizing this firm's work.

To begin with, this image can be said to contain at least two different interacting worlds: that of the house and its reflection in the water. Construction and reflection in a deceptive symmetry which obviously speaks, once again: of at least two realities: that of the actual construction and that of the poetic dream that produces its mirror image. But aren't these two realities exactly the same ones we mentioned in the Foreword when we talked

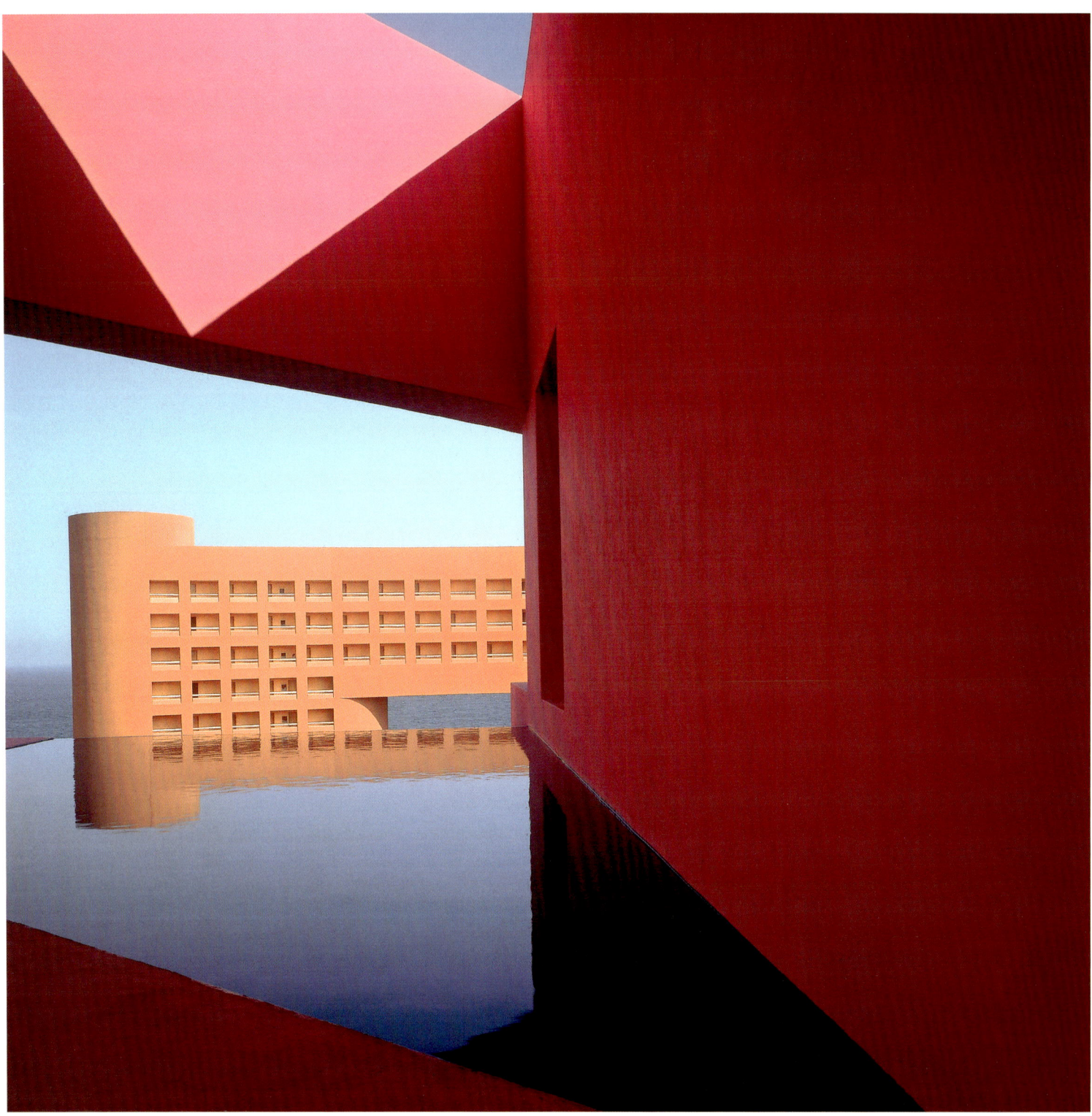

III
THE SPIRIT OF PLACE

THE ENVIRONMENTAL CHALLENGES TODAY'S ARCHITECTURE HAS TO face are enormous. What is taken from the earth to build as well as what is offered in exchange have to be borne increasingly in mind. As Japanese architect Tadao Ando says: "You can't put something new there, just anywhere. First of all, you have to absorb what exists on that particular plot of land, what you can see around it and then you have to use that knowledge, together with a contemporary way of thinking, to interpret what you have seen. De Yturbe Arquitectos shares this way of understanding the land, terrain, environment, landscape and nature. As Enrique Martín-Moreno says, "José de Yturbe's work is a truce between man and nature." The text accompanying the photos and plans of the monograph on De Yturbe Arquitectos work published by L'Arca Edizioni in 1996, entitled *Dwelling versus Building*, also says:

When José de Yturbe approaches a terrain, he does not just see an empty plot of land; the entire design process is subordinated to the existing vegetation and surrounding constructions to make the work seem an integral part of its context.

He allows the vegetation to grow freely and by so doing, it becomes one with the architectural work as they grow old together.

Unfortunately, many people continue to see nature in the same way that English poet William Blake denounced two hundred years ago: "The fool does not see the same tree as the wise man"; at best he sees a nuisance if not simply a pile of wood. It is only with an alert, similar spirit that one can see what Norwegian

27

architect and historian Christian Norberg-Schulz called "the spirit of place" in the late 1970s. In his famous *Genius Loci: Towards a Phenomenology of Modern Architecture*, he explored this idea of *genius loci* in classical antiquity.

According to Norberg-Schulz, all architecture should first of all aspire to transforming its location into an authentic place, revealing the "potential meanings present in a given environment." It should then attempt to understand the nature of the things of the world and listen to what places have to say when "they want to exist" as architect Louis Kahn once said. Le Corbusier himself stated on more than one occasion that architectural emotion is only verified when "the work resounds within us in harmony with the universe, to whose laws we owe obedience, faith and respect." But the universe Le Corbusier speaks of is much more than just the landscape. A place is also a space endowed with a distinctive character: a highly complex, historical, cultural and social phenomenon, in addition to a set of visual considerations.

When we think, to give just one example, of traditional Japanese architecture, we have to think about Japanese culture as a whole and its profound relationship with nature. In Japan, it is still possible to coexist harmoniously with nature, at least in some places. This way of living as part of nature is inseparable from the Japanese way of life, as expressed by Junichiro Tanizaki in his beautiful essay "In Praise of Shadow":

In Japanese houses, the fact that the eaves jut out so far due to the climate, building materials and other factors. For lack, for example, of bricks, glass and cement to protect the walls from sideways gusts of wind, roofs have had to be protected from the front, meaning that the Japanese, who would also have preferred light to a dark dwelling, have been forced to make a virtue out of necessity. But what is generally called beautiful is nothing more than a sublimation of the realities of life which was how our ancestors, forced to live, whether they wanted to or not, in dark dwellings, one day discovered beauty in the depths of shadow and did not take long to use shadow to produce aesthetic effects.

All traditional Japanese architecture is based on these premises. They can be said to be their roots. "Roots are very important," as José de Yturbe, following his master Luis Barragán, says. And it is precisely from this profound connection between human beings and nature that the need arises in great Japanese architecture to integrate the outside and the inside so harmoniously.

The roots of De Yturbe Arquitectos are found, first of all, in the direct teachings of his professors—Barragán, Sordo Madaleno, Villagrán and in the example of the finest 20th century Mexican architects. They are found, by extension, in the traditional way of building houses in Mexico, particularly in the countryside, in both great haciendas and village dwellings. In any case, it is quite clear in De Yturbe Arquitectos work that the process that led them to design interior space—which constitutes inhabitable space as such—precedes the architectural work as sculpture, in other words, as an exterior object. Hence the

Serra, whom he greatly admires, states: "what I normally do is try to submerge myself in all the possible aspects and characteristics of the landscape. But I obviously also want to know how that land has been used, how the sun moves over it and many other things".

The unstoppable process of globalization which, among many other things, obviously affects architecture, at least in terms of the economic conditions under which it is practiced nowadays, led Glenn Murcutt, the unusual Australian architect who won the Pritzker Prize in 2002 to declare:

importance that is always given to the intimacy, privacy and serenity of indoor spaces.

Today, as always, architecture is concerned with people and their living conditions. Although living conditions have changed a great deal, human beings are still human beings and continue to need to relate to the surrounding environment and to coexist harmoniously with "the spirit of the place." Modern architecture cannot exist without this spirit nor would it exist as such. In this respect, architecture today faces the task of closing the gap between the cold logic of technology and science and the spirit of place. De Yturbe Arquitectos fully understands this challenge.

For an architect, the hand is an extension of the brain while the computer is an extension of the hand. De Yturbe does not turn his back on any of the technical innovations architecture has accepted as part of its baggage and language. But the creative process continues to be as mysterious as ever: one either can or cannot see the solution to a space. And among the many solutions available, the most beautiful one—as Le Corbusier said—is the best, regardless of the market's opinion. In the last analysis, as José de Yturbe said about the best way of resolving a project: "There are no rules for me."

The fast pace of modern life, the celerity at which things go out of fashion, the speed of transport, the swiftness of technological discoveries, the pace at which people live, communicate (or fail to), travel, eat, work and even rest leaves its mark on the architectural work of our times. It is no longer possible to wait centuries for a construction to be completed. There's no time any more. But De Yturbe takes his time and in consonance Richard

I am afraid globalization is here to stay. The potential, both negative and positive, is enormous. On the one had, we are becoming a single world, which is very important, but we also face new dangers, because a new form of imperialism might develop in which economic power begins to submerge the true identities of people and places.

That is why for Murcutt, and for all of today's architects, the main problem is that in order to produce quality, authentic architecture, you need time. Like all architects, José de Yturbe complains of the lack of time. "Often," explains De Yturbe, "you spend more time on the contracts than on developing the project to be built." That is the spirit of this age.

However, working while taking into account both the spirit of place and the spirit of the times is absolutely essential for turning construction into art. De Yturbe Arquitectos does not forget this. Mexico in the 21st century. And like a sort of reminder—we will have to use the word again: like an icon—for several decades now, in various projects and palces and with a distinct emphasis each time, this architectural firm has built a characteristic feature: a staircase covered in geraniums, ferns or magueys that has become its sign of identity: the firm's hallmark. Its true signature.

IV

ARCHITECTURE:
THE MAIN WORK

ALTHOUGH IT WOULD SEEM THAT NOWADAYS PEOPLE NO LONGER speak of beauty in the arts, it is essential to discuss this topic in relation to the work of De Yturbe Arquitectos. Because if Barragán's legacy remains alive among his best students, it is because he insists that beauty and aspiring to beauty is a crucial condition for producing real architecture: the main work. A work, if it is really a work of art, is always the main work. That's the point. The work speaks, says and decides. The work dictates what the work needs. And an architect has to know how to listen. In this respect, he resembles a musician. It is no coincidence that Goethe himself referred to architecture as "petrified music." Music consisting of light, air, sight, color, texture, natural beauty and simplicity.

The work of De Yturbe Arquitectos involves, like all architecture, the creation of spaces, but what sets it apart is it has developed the creation of environments to be inhabited without giving up what, for want of a better name, we refer to as "spirituality." And how do you achieve that? I think this can be achieved by designing and constructing spaces that, regardless of their dimensions, give those that live in them and appropriate them a feeling of protection and intimacy. And this is true of both indoor and outdoor spaces: patios, terraces and gardens. Beauty and intimacy.

Except that to achieve this beauty and feeling of intimacy, you need time: time to gestate, develop and complete a work; time that transforms the finishes, patinas and surroundings in which they are inserted and the way we see and experience architectural works; in short, the time required to go through the

33

whole work, as though it were the plot of a comedy or a drama. Let us, then, take the time to tour the house belonging to José de Yturbe, the founder and head of De Yturbe Arquitectos—appreciating it as an icon of his work in that it not only represents but also embodies the virtues of his craftsmanship and puts them to the greatest test of time: their hospitality.

The first thing we can see is a facade which, in its adamant refusal to make any sort of declaration, resembles the silence in which this architect lives most of the time. A man of few words, José de Yturbe lets the construction speak for itself. Crossing the threshold and walking into the house marks the start of a tour that has been deliberately conceived of by José de Yturbe as a stage setting or "architectural strip tease." First of all, we walk down a long narrow passage from which we can see a high strip of sky in which two slender vertical columns rise up, recalling the emblematic works of Barnett Newman which in turn have a distant echo of the Towers of Satélite and the medieval skyscrapers of San Gimignano. As we turn left, the passage leads into an extraordinarily surprising space: an imposing maguey staircase surrounded by orange-colored walls. The firm's hallmark.

Surprise is of course a key feature of contemporary architecture. And although the unexpected constitutes a source of delight for a person seeing the house for the first time, the house has enough substance and enigma to be able to surprise the permanent inhabitants of this space on a daily basis. Like all surprising architectural spaces, this one has been consciously planned, bearing in mind both the limitations the state places on constructions in this part of Mexico City (at least five meters free of construction at the front) and the architect's personal and family history. "My family owned a pulque hacienda in Tlaxcala."

Once we have recovered from the surprise of this staircase of giant plants, green stars that are so reminiscent of the paintings of Pedro Diego de Alvarado, Diego Rivera's grandson, we come across immense amphoras for storing oil which from the moment we see them, say: this space acknowledges its debt to Luis Barragán's settings. Brought from Mérida to stand guard next to the following landmark in the construction: a feature that completely overshadows the surprise of the passage and the first courtyard: an impressive door weighing two tons, carved out of volcanic rock from the Popocatépetl (known as "recinto" meaning "enclosure") which swings open apparently effortlessly to welcome you into the house.

What first meets our eyes is a circular hall overlooked by a golden triptych. The painting immediately recalls another icon by Mathias Goeritz that dominates José de Yturbe's office except that this time, more than an icon, it is actually an iconostasis. An iconostasis is a screen with painted sacred images, with three doors, a large one in the center flanked by two smaller ones, separating the presbytery and its altar from the rest of the church. Except that in this case, the presbytery is open and no images.

Opposite the iconstatis stand three large silvery glass spheres, like those of which Chucho Reyes Ferreira was so fond.

others. "For example, in the Ronchamp chapel," Gerzso used to say, "Le Corbusier made an apple [assuming that all painters and visual artists have painted apples at some time in their lives] in a different, extremely impressive way."

José de Yturbe has painted his apple, so to speak, in his own, inimitable style, without ever turning his back on his aesthetic family, yet without stopping to look back when the time came to make decisions and resolve a space or a project. The courtyard, large, smooth walls, spectacular volumes and tucks, the colors drawn from Mexican popular art, the enormous windows, water mirrors, the echo of pyramdis and provincial haciendas, bear out what has been said.

The three spheres obviously recall the three guardian spirits of the office, present at the entry to his house: Luis Barragán, Mathias Goeritz, and Jesús Reyes Ferreira. Part of the beauty of this space and the elements that lend it character is obviously due to the fact that the elements are unexpected, like the floor of the hall: a replica of an old floor taken from a Syrian construction, which, with its discreet, precise geometry underlines the aesthetic quality of the lessons of his teachers as well as José de Yturbe's approach to building, which is determined to renew this tradition.

The hall leads into a spacious spiral staircase linking the two main floors of the residence which, since it was built on a beautiful ravine in Lomas de Chapultepec, has quite naturally adopted a pyramidal distribution. As we explore the house, the woodwork emerges as a key feature: floors and furniture complement each other, sharing not only an aesthetic, but an ethic: that the hand of the man that made this furniture should be felt and that local materials should hold pride of place.

Thus we move into a large circular library overlooking a courtyard from which it is possible to observe the pyramidal structure of the house as well as the vertical features we glimpsed from the entrance passage. From this perspective, they can be seen for what they really are: large slabs of color that immediately recall the spaces Gunther Gerzso used to construct in his paintings. A triangular fountain complements the courtyard from which one can see the cloudless blue sky. "We are in another world."

Except that these words by the architect himself remind me of others by poet Paul Eluard who used to say: "yes, there is another world: it's this one." And just as some words remind me of others, José de Yturbe's house recalls other houses and constructions, since there is no work of art that is not based on

In José de Yturbe's house, the legacy of Mexican architecture and art is reflected in the extraordinary drawings by Orozco, the delicate craftsmanship of Gerzso and García Guerrero and the colors and strength of the paintings by Pedro Coronel and Dr. Atl.

Because, after all, and as Goeritz said in "Manifesto of Emotional Architecture" nowadays, "asking for more than a nice, pleasant, adequate house means asking for spiritual elevation."

Nowadays, beauty continues to fulfill the same function as ever: Extolling life. Making life worthy to be lived as human beings. Facilitating harmony with the environment and all other beings, including, of course, all other human beings. That is something that goes far beyond mere appearances. It is something that goes beyond eyes, sight and the senses. It's architecture.

AFTERWORD

Stop looking at architecture
that traces the fire of artifice
In August skies. It contains the vices
of all human creatures:

The vice of not lasting. The dazzling building
only lasts for a second
leaving us the sacred benefit
Of a light on a dark night.

Come . . . Look for what is most durable.
This summer night has turned on
its innumerable lights in the heights for you:

be silent and let her speak.
And from the fleeting shooting stars simply learn
to prepare your divine leap.

Pedro Salinas

Midi le juste y compose de feux
La mer, la mer, toujours recommencée!
O récompense après une pensée
Qu'un long regard sur le calme des dieux!

PAUL VALÉRY

41

Architecture is life, or at least it is life
itself taking form and therefore it is the
truest record of life as it was lived in
the world yesterday, as it is lived today
or ever will be lived.

FRANK LLOYD WRIGHT

Light is my steed in battle.

ALBERTO BLANCO

I have what I once did not have:
　　　　Lots of blue with little clouds.
　　　　The sun wants this calm
　　　　　　　　to be the supreme palm.
Walls.
Tailored
Garden
　　　　　asks the rest to be forgotten.

JORGE GUILLÉN

The wind sculpts the stone,
the stone is a goblet of water,
water escapes and is wind.
Stone, wind, water.
    The swirling winds sing,
    the rippling water murmurs,
    the immobile stone remains silent.
    Wind, water, stone.

OCTAVIO PAZ

Bear perspective in mind. Large things
are clearly large, but small things can also
be so when seen close up.

Shiki

Paolo Uccello did not execute paintings in
which he did not add new light to the art
of perspective, whether in buildings or
in colonnades, which in a shallow
field feign ample space.

LUIGI LANZI

61

There resides the candor that today
illuminates us with three flames.

César Vallejo

And when the cupboard's bare
I'll still find something there
with my love.

Paul McCartney

The third type of straight line is the diagonal, which schematically divides the horizontal and vertical into equal angles. Its tendency toward both lines is equivalent, which makes its inner tone: the meeting of cold and hot. In other words, the cleanest form of infinite, temperate movement.

WASSILY KANDINSKY

Beauty, as wisdom,
loves the solitary worshipper.

LUIS BARRAGÁN

71

We are the stage for everything
we have seen.

Isamu Noguchi

Purity of form, the beauty of forms are
forms – independently, that is, of subjects or
intentions. We must hold to the principle
that in art beauty is the sole legitimate
criterion – and the only one that keeps its
effectiveness.

MARIE-ALAIN COUTURIER

External limitations may stimulate our
inventiveness instead of limiting it.
We need this sort of flexibility in times
of crisis. We take pride in knowledge
and we forget that events only
reflect light.

ANNI ALBERS

Blue does not produce any real
representation of the infinite. One might
say sight rays strike a cupola and they cannot
penetrate the infinite. The suprematist white
infinity allows for rays of sight to advance
without encountering any limit. We can
see bodies in movement.

KAZIMIR MALÉVICH

Philosophy, poetry, architecture want to make our world habitable.

Ramón Xirau

There is a classicist at odds with a
romantic in all Mexican artists, writers,
and politicians. The fixed, ordered,
rational, symmetrical image is constantly
assailed by the image of the unruly,
of disorder, intuition, and dreams.

CARLOS FUENTES

The rooms, the stairways, which were
descending with ceremonious slow steps,
other stairways . . .

RAINER MARIA RILKE

As the afternoon fell
The two or three colors of the patio lay down to rest.
Tonight, the moon, the light circle,
does not dominate its space.
Patio, channeled sky.
The patio is the slanting incline
through which the sky pours itself into the house.
Serene,
eternity awaits at the starry crossroads.
It is pleasant to live in the dark friendship of an entryway,
a grapevine, and a pool.

Jorge Luis Borges

The afternoon falls
    on the roof tiles
    and it falls . . .
Who gave it wings to come
    swooping down?

PABLO NERUDA

Red earth, completely virgin earth
impregnated by the most generous blood,
earth where human life has no
price, it is always spread out, like the
maguey that stretches toward the horizon
and represents it, to be consumed in a
flower of desire and danger.

ANDRÉ BRETON

The limit is the true protagonist of space
as the present; the other limit is the true
protagonist of time.

EDUARDO CHILLIDA

By cutting out doors and windows we
build a house and on that which is
non-existent [on the empty space within]
depends the house's utility.

Therefore, existence renders actual,
but non-existence renders useful.

LAO TSE, *TAO TE CHING*

As line, the straight line; as form,
the rectangle; primary colors; a pure
and simple organization of space.

PIET MONDRIAN

123

Development, and finally the
predomination of the abstract element,
is natural, because no matter how much
the organic form recedes, the more it
shifts to the foreground and the abstract
form gains in resonance.

WASSILY KANDINSKY

I am sick and tired, above all, of the artificial and hysterical atmosphere of the so-called art world with their adulterated pleasures. I would like a chair to be a chair, as simple as that, without all the sick mystification invented around it.

MATHIAS GOERITZ

Finally, we have in our sitting rooms that hollow space called *toko no ma* that we adorn with a painting or a floral decoration: but the essential function of that image or of those flowers is not decorative in itself, instead it is a matter of adding dimension in the sense of depth to the shadow. In selecting the painting to put there, the first thing we seek is harmony with the walls of the *toko no ma*, which we call *toko-utsuri*. For the same reason, we regard its placement with importance on part with the graphic value of the calligraphic inscription or the drawing, because a *toko-utsuri* lacking harmony would deprive the most indisputable masterpiece of all interest.

JUNICHIRO TANIZAKI

Practice has shown me that to bring
out the joy of white, it is necessary
to surround it with the powerful
rumor of colors.

LE CORBUSIER

133

The wooden temple reaches perfection the
more it is stripped, lacking adornment
it is the space that embraces you . . .

ITALO CALVINO

It is the task of the architect and
the contemporary artist to attempt to
imbue their era with spirituality . . .

Mathias Goeritz

I'm not interested in people following my work or making work like my work. But what does interest me is the notion that if you do a lot of work it means there's a potential for other people to understand that a lot of things are possible with a sustained effort and that the broadening of experiences is possible and I think that's all art can be. A little catalyst for change.

RICHARD SERRA

The house is in the sea,
full of spume.
The house clashes and turns into white
A lesson in courtesy:
For what was a reef.

Braulio Arenas

145

We have worked with the hope that our
labor serves in tandem in the great task
of dignifying human life on the paths of
beauty and contributes to raising a
dike against the breaking waves of
dehumanization and vulgarity.

LUIS BARRAGÁN

White acts as our soul as a great absolute silence . . . it is a silence that is not dead, but rather, on the contrary, full of living possibilities. White sounds like a silence that soon can be understood.

WASSILY KANDINSKY

Knowing yourself is the open door.

KRISHNAMURTI

153

Less is more.

Ludwig Mies van der Rohe

157

I always imagined Paradise would be some
kind of library . . .

Jorge Luis Borges

This proves for the reading of color what
Kandinsky often demanded for the
reading of art: what counts is not
the what but the how.

JOSEPH ALBERS

No house should ever be on a hill or
on anything. It should be of the hill.
Belonging to it. Hill and house should live
together each the happier for the other.

FRANK LLOYD WRIGHT

When Ricardo Legorreta asked Walter Gropius once where to go in order to do graduate studies in architecture, Gropius asked him, "Where do you want to practice?" Legorreta replied: "Mexico." "Then go to Mexico," was Gropius's advice.

ANTHONY C. ANTONIADES

For the artist, communication with nature
continues to be the essential condition.
The artist is human; he himself, nature;
part of nature within the space of nature.

Paul Klee

In dreams and in wakefulness, the sweet
memory of marvelous fountains have
accompanied me all through my life:
those that will eternally mark my
childhood, those spills of waters
overflowing from dams, pools on
haciendas, over those stones around
wells in monastery courtyards; the
trenches where water runs joyfully . . .

LUIS BARRAGÁN

Most people don't care much about
architecture itself, but what matters is
their reaction to space. I like this reaction.

RENZO PIANO

Buildings, too, are children of Earth and Sun.

FRANK LLOYD WRIGHT

Without the void, there is nothing to be done. It is the great pit from which help for everything can be pulled out, in spatial volumes that speak, and that clearly speak, whether they are positive or negative.

EDUARDO CHILLIDA

These sculpted spaces are the shrine,
the virtuous housing that calls for the
senses to meld in spirit.

THE MEXICAN ARCHITECTURAL FIRM,
DE YTURBE ARQUITECTOS

IGOR MORENO

TWO MAJOR PROTAGONISTS ARE INVOLVED IN ARCHITECTURE: THE person who designs the spaces and the one who lives in them. In the normal course of events, we concentrate on the one who does the planning, since it is this person's genius and inventiveness that lead to the creation of spaces acclaimed for their plasticity and functionality. The most commonly used method of making an architect's work known is photography, while some books on architecture also include floor plans and perhaps a technical explanation as well, to enable readers to better understand the distribution of spaces or the details of the building solution applied.

However, only rarely do we dedicate a few lines to documenting the testimony of those who live within the architecture, of those who proposed an architectural program and journeyed together with the architect over the difficult road to the completion of the project. Obviously, these feelings cannot be photographed. Starting from the premise that architecture is a quest to change the way we live and to modify humanity's very manner of interacting with their environment, we then proceed to commit ourselves to the task of determining—in a way that goes beyond a mere array of photographs—whether this task has been accomplished.

In architecture, the experience of penetrating spaces is comparable to the importance in literature of reading different authors. In so doing, we can discern the architect's language and, walking through these paths alter our senses, to a greater or lesser degree, by the magic of the place. Giving

219

voice to this occurrence, when spaces charm us, inexorably leads us to poetry.

The experience of living in a De Yturbe house is one where the boundary between serenity and silence is blurred, where perception is enchanted by temporality. Mystery as seen here is the firstness that connects with manifold and ancient memories that finally evoke nostalgia and even border on melancholy.

The spaces are not gratuitous. They are the absolute decision of a language that has an urgency which, we might say, supplies the needed inspiration. Common sense, serenity, and wisdom, the forward-looking kind, incite nature to let itself be entrapped by magic and aroma.

A José de Yturbe house always involves the promenade, where walking is perceived as an aesthetic practice. The dweller strolls around, letting himself be swayed by the sensual rhythm of the architectural language, by the guileless senses that are part of him. Full of surprises, every single walk to and fro is a permanently changing experience.

A quiet reflecting pool is an inevitable component of his courtyards, the mirror of passing moments, the reflection that absorbs time like the memory of what is unearthed.

Color is the captivating skin that sheathes the walls. The chronicle of the seasons. Intense and definite. Mexican.

A De Yturbe house is filled with joy, it is a vortex of energy, a promise kept with the eloquent passing of the sun overhead. The penumbra is ephemeral. We discover in these dwellings that truth lies somewhere between sunlight and shade. The moon, when it appears, reveals itself to very few — to the inhabitants — at precise times, when the sun has decamped. Thus, the praise of shade is permanent.

And so, no photograph can capture the experience of penetrating the spaces sculpted by the architect's genius.

José de Yturbe's architecture could perhaps mistakenly be considered a nostalgic view of vernacular architecture. One should avoid falling into this trap. It is much more complex. It relates to a formal proposition about harmony. It leads the dwellers to pay attention through their senses, it leads them to understand the message, so that it is a natural process for them to learn what is needed and to order this map. It is an overall perception that wisely lets in magic, mystery and shelter. Architecture here provokes the psyche; it is a place where coming in means escaping.

The work of DYA shows enormous respect for — and actually higlights — the signs of temporality on a site. There is no plagiarizing. It understands and joins in harmony the tensions demanded by the spaces. It is an architecture that, as Adolf Loos intuitively perceived, rejects all opprobrious ornament on principle.

In an era where the language of construction is eliminating all thick lines from drawings — almost in desperation, it would seem — and thus must face the challenge of materializ-

possibly best synthesizes his architectural thinking. The reverence for the site is absolute; the 16th, 18th and 19th centuries are captured, they are all there, past, present and future melded in Kayros.

DYA works such as Casa Los Eucaliptos comprise an architectural legacy. It condenses the languages of fine arts into one. It is a collection of harmonies and covenants that decant the spirit. Its semantic content, therefore, finds surprising parallels with Le Corbusier's Villa Savoye or his Citrohan House.

ing the finest line, De Yturbe avoids falling into the temptation of this particular form of being modern.

At the dawn of the new century, man, displaying immaculate individualism, detached from all contact with nature, seeks to expose himself at all costs, as if to assert that he lives, that he is. Today, the all-glass dwelling of the 21st century seems to have become the reality show of each person caught in his own labyrinth of solitude. Blinds, ever shut, have gradually come to symbolize the subdued paranoia brought about by the inexplicable absence of the protective wall.

We withdraw from the sun, thus detracting from the quality of our days. Inhibited introspection, engendered by architecture that has seemingly forgotten its raison d'être, thrusts man away from bliss.

By walking through spaces, in remembrance of things past, one could cite three Mexican architectural works of the 20th century that fulfill their task of leading human beings to a state of rapture: the Barragán House, where man's spirituality is extolled; the Capuchin Convent, where the presence of a supreme being is glorified; and finally, the Casona de Chimalistac (The Mansion in Chimalistac), where the experience of wandering through its grounds brings on a sense of melancholy that makes you yearn for childhood and go back in time to a past scented with orange blossoms.

And so, just as there is music we want to hear time and again because of its beauty, because of the way it can enthrall and change us, so do these three works seem to patiently await our return, always.

In the Casona de Chimalistac, De Yturbe offers us one of his most brilliant creations. Exquisite. This is the work that

The work created by De Yturbe Arquitectos is an exercise in synthesis, one that brings order to the environment, provides enjoyment, and expresses social and cultural norms. Although it doesn't imitate the past, nor does it break with tradition. It is an architecture that transcends the purely practical to give way to an experience of syncretism, where thoughts and feelings merge, to transform the person that dwells in its spaces into a better human being.

IGOR MORENO©
A dweller in architecture

CURRICULUM VITAE

JOSÉ DE YTURBE BERNAL WAS BORN IN 1942 IN MEXICO CITY. HE STUDIED CIVIL ENGINEERING from 1961 to 1963 when he transferred to the School of Architecture of the Universidad Iberoamericana (UIA) in Mexico City. He received his Architecture degree from the UIA in 1969. In 1968 he began his private practice. In 1969 he worked with the design team of Luigi W. Moretti in Rome, Italy, and returned in 1970 to lead a very prominent private practice in Mexico City. During that time, demand for his architectural designs grew, with the results of such projects as the Torre Alta in Monterrey, Nuevo León, which won him first prize in the Mexican Architectural Biennial in 1985, with the completion of the Westin Regina Hotels in Puerto Vallarta and Los Cabos* in 1993, and the Malinalco Golf Clubhouse* also in 1993 along with more than 180 other projects, mainly residential.

In 1992 he was selected by the Mexican Council for Arts and Culture (CONACULTA) as one of the six architects for the development of the National Arts Center. He presented a preliminary Master Plan for the whole complex and then was involved in the development of the movie theater area of the project.

In 1997 José de Yturbe attended the "Golf Course Design" and the "Golf Clubhouse Design and Site Planning" courses at the Harvard Graduate School of Design. That same year he was also invited for a "Master Builder" Distinguished Professorship at Florida Atlantic University.

José de Yturbe has lectured in several universities in Mexico and the United States. In October 1997 he was invited by the International Society for the Fostering of Architectural Culture (FICA) to be part of the 12th International Congress "Prophecies for the 21st Century". His lecture was viewed by over 90,000 people world wide. In 1998 he was admitted as a member of the Mexican Academy of Architecture.

In 1999 José de Yturbe began his career as a Golf Course Architect with the design of an 18-hole golf club, the Nejapa Country Club in Managua, Nicaragua. During its more than 30-year history, De Yturbe Arquitectos has gained critical acclaim both in Mexico and abroad, opening the doors to international commissions, mainly in the United States and Central America. Its works have been published all over the world.

JOSÉ DE YTURBE SORDO was born in México City in 1972. He studied architecture at the Anahuac University in 1998, and afterwards a Master's in Business Administration (MBA) at the Instituto de Empresa in Madrid (2002). He has worked in different firms in Mexico and the United States. He has been a partner at De Yturbe Arquitectos since 2003.

ANDRÉS CAJIGA RAMÍREZ was born in Mexico City in 1970. He studied architecture from 1988 to 1993 at the Universidad Iberoamericana. After graduating he worked with architect Alberto Rimoch and afterwards with Sordo Madaleno Associates. Since 1993, has been Project Director at De Yturbe Arquitectos designing, developing, coordinating and supervising different projects.

*In partnership with Javier Sordo Madaleno.

Casa de Los Magueyes, 1996
Mexico City, Mexico
Photo © *Fernando Cordero*
p. 5

The Westin Resort & Spa, 1989
Cabo San Lucas,
San Lucas, BCS, Mexico
Photo © *Fernando Cordero*
p. 22

Hacienda Santa Rosa, 2003
Valle de Bravo,
State of Mexico, Mexico
Photo © *Fernando Cordero*
p. 37

Casa El Sabino, 1997
Valle de Bravo,
State of Mexico, Mexico
Photo © *Alfonso de Béjar*
p. 44

Caballeriza Los Manantiales, 2008
Valle de Bravo,
State of Mexico, Mexico
Photo © *Michael Calderwood*
pp. 8, 176

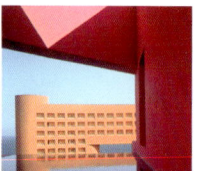

The Westin Resort & Spa, 1989
Cabo San Lucas,
San Lucas, BCS, Mexico
Photo © *Fernando Cordero*
p. 26

Club de Golf Malinalco, 1993
Malinalco,
State of Mexico, Mexico
Photo © *Fernando Cordero*
p. 40

Casa El Sabino, 1997
Valle de Bravo,
State of Mexico, Mexico
Photo © *Alfonso de Béjar*
p. 45

Casa Masri, 1998
Valle de Bravo,
State of Mexico, Mexico
Photo © *Paul Czitrom*
p. 10

Casa del Lago, 2003
Valle de Bravo,
State of Mexico, Mexico
Photo © *Michael Calderwood*
p. 31

Costa Baja Resort & Spa, 2004
La Paz, BCS, Mexico
Photo © *Michael Calderwood*
p. 41

Casa El Sabino, 1997
Valle de Bravo,
State of Mexico, Mexico
Photo © *Fernando Cordero*
p. 46

Casa Las Palmas 1, 2002
Punta Mita, Nayarit, Mexico
Photo © *Miguel García*
p. 14

Casa Las Palmas 1, 2002
Punta Mita, Nayarit, Mexico
Photo © *Fernando Cordero*
p. 32

Casa El Sabino, 1997
Valle de Bravo,
State of Mexico, Mexico
Photo © *Fernando Cordero*
p. 42

Casa Las Palmas 1, 2002
Punta Mita, Nayarit, Mexico
Photo © *Fernando Cordero*
p. 47

Caballerizas Hacienda Santa Rosa, 2007
Valle de Bravo,
State of Mexico, Mexico
Photo © *Michael Calderwood*
p. 18

Casa Uno, 1968
Valle de Bravo,
State of Mexico, Mexico
Photo © *Fernando Cordero*
p. 36

Casa de Los Espejos, 2000
Valle de Bravo,
State of Mexico, Mexico
Photo © *Fernando Cordero*
p. 43

Casa de Los Patios, 2006
El Bajío, Mexico
Photo © *Fernando Cordero*
p. 48

Casa de Los Patios, 2006
El Bajío, Mexico
Photo © *Fernando Cordero*
p. 49

Casa de Los Patios, 1998-2006
El Bajío, Mexico
Photo © *Fernando Cordero*
p. 56

Casa de Los Patios, 1998-2006
El Bajío, Mexico
Photo © *Fernando Cordero*
p. 61

Casa de Los Espejos, 2000
Valle de Bravo,
State of Mexico, Mexico
Photo © *Alfonso de Béjar*
p. 67

Casa de Los Patios, 2006
El Bajío, Mexico
Photo © *Fernando Cordero*
pp. 50, 51

Casa de Los Patios, 1998-2006
El Bajío, Mexico
Photo © *Fernando Cordero*
p. 57

Casa de Los Patios, 1998-2006
El Bajío, Mexico
Photo © *Fernando Cordero*
p. 62

Hacienda Santa Rosa, 2003
Valle de Bravo,
State of Mexico, Mexico
Photo © *Fernando Cordero*
p. 67

Casa de Los Patios, 2006
El Bajío, Mexico
Photo © *Fernando Cordero*
p. 52

Casa en Bezares, 2003
Mexico City, Mexico
Photo © *Fernando Cordero*
p. 58

Casa de Los Patios, 1998-2006
El Bajío, Mexico
Photo © *Fernando Cordero*
p. 63

Casa El Sabino, 1997
Valle de Bravo,
State of Mexico, Mexico
Photo © *Fernando Cordero*
p. 67

Casa de Los Patios, 2006
El Bajío, Mexico
Photo © *Fernando Cordero*
p. 53

Casa en Bezares, 2003
Mexico City, Mexico
Photo © *Fernando Cordero*
p. 59

Casa de Los Patios, 1998-2006
El Bajío, Mexico
Photo © *Fernando Cordero*
pp. 64, 65

Club de Golf Izar, 1995
Valle de Bravo,
State of Mexico, Mexico
Photo © *Alfonso de Béjar*
p. 67

Casa de Los Patios, 2006
El Bajío, Mexico
Photo © *Fernando Cordero*
pp. 54, 55

Casa de Los Patios, 1998-2006
El Bajío, Mexico
Photo © *Fernando Cordero*
p. 60

Casa sy, 1994
Valle de Bravo,
State of Mexico, Mexico
Photo © *Arturo Zavala Haag*
p. 66

Casa de Los Espejos, 2000
Valle de Bravo,
State of Mexico, Mexico
Photo © *Fernando Cordero*
p. 68

Casa Las Palmas 2, 2002
Punta Mita, Nayarit, Mexico
Photo © *Fernando Cordero*
p. 69

Casa de Los Patios, 1998-2006
El Bajío, Mexico
Photo © *Fernando Cordero*
p. 74

Casa de Los Cilindros, 2001
Valle de Bravo,
State of Mexico, Mexico
Photo © *Fernando Cordero*
p. 80

Conjunto 11, 2004
Mexico City, Mexico
Photo © *Fernando Cordero*
p. 85

Casa Celosía, 2006
Cancún, Quintana Roo,
Mexico
Photo © *Michael Calderwood*
p. 70

Casa de Los Patios, 1998-2006
El Bajío, Mexico
Photo © *Fernando Cordero*
p. 75

Casa de Los Cilindros, 2001
Valle de Bravo,
State of Mexico, Mexico
Photo © *Luis Gordoa*
p. 81

Casa de Los Eucaliptos, 1998
Mexico City, Mexico
Photo © *Alfonso de Béjar*
p. 86

Casa El Sabino, 2001
Valle de Bravo,
State of Mexico, Mexico
Photo © *Fernando Cordero*
p. 71

Casa de Los Patios, 1998-2006
El Bajío, Mexico
Photo © *Fernando Cordero*
pp. 76, 77

Casa de Los Patios, 1998-2006
El Bajío, Mexico
Photo © *Fernando Cordero*
p. 82

Casa de Los Eucaliptos, 1998
Mexico City, Mexico
Photo © *Alfonso de Béjar*
p. 87

Casa 8 x, 1994
Valle de Bravo,
State of Mexico, Mexico
Photo © *Arturo Zavala Haag*
p. 72

Casa en Bezares, 2003
Mexico City, Mexico
Photo © *Fernando Cordero*
p. 78

Casa en Bezares, 2003
Mexico City, Mexico
Photo © *Fernando Cordero*
p. 83

Conjunto 11, 2004
Mexico City, Mexico
Photo © *Fernando Cordero*
p. 64

Casa Las Palmas 2, 2002
Punta Mita, Nayarit, Mexico
Photo © *Fernando Cordero*
p. 73

Casa de Los Patios, 1998-2006
El Bajío, Mexico
Photo © *Fernando Cordero*
p. 79

Conjunto 11, 2004
Mexico City, Mexico
Photo © *Fernando Cordero*
p. 84

Conjunto 11, 2004
Mexico City, Mexico
Photo © *Fernando Cordero*
p. 89

Casa de Los Magueyes, 1996
Mexico City, Mexico
Photo © Fernando Cordero
p. 90

Rancho Los Manantiales, 2002
Valle de Bravo,
State of Mexico, Mexico
Photo © Fernando Cordero
p. 95

Casa de Los Eucaliptos, 1998
State of Mexico, Mexico
Photo © Alfonso de Béjar
p. 100

Hacienda Santa Rosa, 2003
Valle de Bravo,
State of Mexico, Mexico
Photo © Fernando Cordero
p. 105

Casa Fuentes, 1973
Mexico City, Mexico
Photo © Fernando Cordero
p. 91

Casa de Los Magueyes, 1996
Mexico City, Mexico
Photo © Fernando Cordero
p. 96

Casa de Los Eucaliptos, 1998
State of Mexico, Mexico
Photo © Alfonso de Béjar
p. 101

Club de Golf Malinalco, 1993
Malinalco,
State of Mexico, Mexico
Photo © Fernando Cordero
p. 106

Hacienda Santa Rosa, 2003
Valle de Bravo,
State of Mexico, Mexico
Photo © Fernando Cordero
p. 92

Casa de Los Magueyes, 1996
Mexico City, Mexico
Photo © Fernando Cordero
p. 97

Casa de Los Magueyes, 1996
Mexico City, Mexico
Photo © Fernando Cordero
p. 102

Club de Golf Malinalco, 1993
Malinalco,
State of Mexico, Mexico
Photo © Fernando Cordero
p. 107

Casa El Sabino, 1997
Valle de Bravo,
State of Mexico, Mexico
Photo © Fernando Cordero
p. 93

Casa de Los Magueyes, 1996
Mexico City, Mexico
Photo © Fernando Cordero
p. 98

Casa de Los Magueyes, 1996
Mexico City, Mexico
Photo © Fernando Cordero
p. 103

Casa de Los Magueyes, 1996
Mexico City, Mexico
Photo © Fernando Cordero
p. 108

Casa de Los Espejos, 2000
Valle de Bravo,
State of Mexico, Mexico
Photo © Fernando Cordero
p. 94

Casa de Los Magueyes, 1996
Mexico City, Mexico
Photo © Fernando Cordero
p. 99

Hacienda Santa Rosa, 2003
Valle de Bravo,
State of Mexico, Mexico
Photo © Fernando Cordero
p. 104

Casa de Los Magueyes, 1996
Mexico City, Mexico
Photo © Fernando Cordero
p. 108

Casa de Los Magueyes, 1996
Mexico City, Mexico
Photo © *Fernando Cordero*
p. 108

Casa Cascada, 1974
Mexico City, Mexico
Photo © *Fernando Cordero*
p. 113

Conjunto Izar 2, 1999
Valle de Bravo,
State of Mexico, Mexico
Photo © *Fernando Cordero*
p. 118

Nejapa Golf Country Club, 1999
Managua, Nicaragua
Photo © *Alfonso de Béjar*
p. 122

Casa de Los Magueyes, 1996
Mexico City, Mexico
Photo © *Fernando Cordero*
p. 108

Casa de Los Cilindros, 1994
Valle de Bravo,
State of Mexico, Mexico
Photo © *Fernando Cordero*
p. 114

Rancho Los Manantiales, 2002
Valle de Bravo,
State of Mexico, Mexico
Photo © *Fernando Cordero*
p. 119

Casa de Los Patios, 2004
El Bajío, Mexico
Photo © *Fernando Cordero*
p. 123

Casa de Los Magueyes, 1996
Mexico City, Mexico
Photo © *Fernando Cordero*
p. 109

Casa s y, 1994
Valle de Bravo,
State of Mexico, Mexico
Photo © *Fernando Cordero*
p. 115

Hacienda Santa Rosa, 2003
Valle de Bravo,
State of Mexico, Mexico
Photo © *Fernando Cordero*
p. 120

Casa Palma Real, 1998
Managua, Nicaragua
Foto © *Alfonso de Béjar*
p. 124

Casa de Los Cilindros, 2001
Valle de Bravo,
State of Mexico, Mexico
Photo © *Fernando Cordero*
pp. 110, 111

Casa del Lago, 2003
Valle de Bravo,
State of Mexico, Mexico
Photo © *Michael Calderwood*
p. 116

Casa El Sabino, 1997
Valle de Bravo,
State of Mexico, Mexico
Photo © *Fernando Cordero*
p. 121

Casa Palma Real, 1998
Managua, Nicaragua
Photo © *Alfonso de Béjar*
p. 125

Casa de Los Espejos, 2000
Valle de Bravo,
State of Mexico, Mexico
Photo © *Fernando Cordero*
p. 112

Casa Celosía, 2006
Cancún, Quintana Roo,
Mexico
Photo © *Michael Calderwood*
p. 117

Hacienda Santa Rosa, 2003
Valle de Bravo,
State of Mexico, Mexico
Photo © *Fernando Cordero*
p. 121

Casa Palma Real, 1998
Managua, Nicaragua
Photo © *Alfonso de Béjar*
p. 125

Casa S Y, 1994
Valle de Bravo,
State of Mexico, Mexico
Photo © *Arturo Zavala Haag*
p. 126

Casa Los Manantiales 1, 2002
Valle de Bravo,
State of Mexico, Mexico
Photo © *Fernando Cordero*
p. 130

Club de Golf Izar, 2000
Valle de Bravo,
State of Mexico, Mexico
Photo © *Fernando Cordero*
p. 135

Casa Cascada, 1972
Mexico City, Mexico
Photo © *Fernando Cordero*
p. 137

Casa Cascada, 1972
Mexico City, Mexico
Photo © *Fernando Cordero*
p. 127

Hacienda Santa Rosa, 2003
Valle de Bravo,
State of Mexico, Mexico
Photo © *Fernando Cordero*
p. 131

Casa Granizo, 1974
Mexico City, Mexico
Photo © *Fernando Cordero*
p. 136

Hacienda Santa Rosa, 2003
Valle de Bravo,
State of Mexico, Mexico
Photo © *Fernando Cordero*
p. 138

Casa Los Manantiales 2, 2002
Valle de Bravo,
State of Mexico, Mexico
Photo © *Fernando Cordero*
p. 128

Casa Las Palmas 1, 2002
Punta Mita, Nayarit, Mexico
Photo © *Fernando Cordero*
p. 132

Casa Granizo, 1974
Mexico City, Mexico
Photo © *Fernando Cordero*
p. 136

Casa Cascada, 1972
Mexico City, Mexico
Photo © *Fernando Cordero*
p. 139

Casa Los Manantiales 2, 2002
Valle de Bravo,
State of Mexico, Mexico
Photo © *Fernando Cordero*
p. 129

Casona Chimalistac, 1984
Mexico City, Mexico
Photo © *Mario Mutschlechner*
p. 133

Casa Granizo, 1974
Mexico City, Mexico
Photo © *Fernando Cordero*
p. 136

Hacienda Santa Rosa, 2003
Valle de Bravo,
State of Mexico, Mexico
Photo © *Fernando Cordero*
p. 139

Casa Girault, 1982
Mexico City, Mexico
Photo © *Archivo D*
Arquitectos
p. 129

Club de Golf Izar, 2000
Valle de Bravo,
State of Mexico, Mexico
Photo © *Fernando Cordero*
p. 134

Casa Granizo, 1974
Mexico City, Mexico
Photo © *Fernando Cordero*
p. 136

Club de Golf Nejapa, 1999
Managua, Nicaragua
Photo © *Alfonso de Béjar*
p. 140

Casa S Y, 1994
Valle de Bravo,
State of Mexico, Mexico
Photo © *Arturo Zavala Haag*
p. 141

Casa Los Manantiales 1, 2002
Valle de Bravo,
State of Mexico, Mexico
Photo © *Fernado Cordero*
p. 146

Rancho Huracán, 1989
Nayarit, Mexico
Photo © *Fernado Cordero*
p. 151

Casa de Los Espejos, 2000
Valle de Bravo,
State of Mexico, Mexico
Photo © *Alfonso de Béjar*
p. 153

Casa del Lago, 2003
Valle de Bravo,
State of Mexico, Mexico
Photo © *Michael Calderwood*
p. 142

Hacienda Santa Rosa, 2003
Valle de Bravo,
State of Mexico, Mexico
Photo © *Fernando Cordero*
p. 147

Casa de Los Magueyes, 1996
Mexico City, Mexico
Photo © *Undine Prohl*
p. 152

Casa Celosía, 2006
Cancún, Quintana Roo, Mexico
Photo © *Michael Calderwood*
p. 154

Casona Chimalistac, 1990
Condumex, Mexico City,
Mexico
Photo © *Michael Calderwood*
p. 143

Casa del Lago, 2003
Valle de Bravo,
State of Mexico, Mexico
Photo © *Michael Calderwood*
p. 148

Casa de Los Magueyes, 1996
Mexico City, Mexico
Photo © *Fernando Cordero*
p. 152

Casa del Lago, 2003
Valle de Bravo,
State of Mexico, Mexico
Photo © *Michael Calderwood*
p. 155

Casa de Los Magueyes, 1996
Mexico City, Mexico
Photo © *Fernando Cordero*
p. 144

Casa del Lago, 2003
Valle de Bravo,
State of Mexico, Mexico
Photo © *Michael Calderwood*
p. 149

Casa de Los Magueyes, 1996
Mexico City, Mexico
Photo © *Undine Prohl*
p. 152

Casa Celosía, 2006
Cancún, Quintana Roo, Mexico
Photo © *Michael Calderwood*
p. 156

Casa Las Palmas 2, 2002
Punta Mita, Nayarit, Mexico
Photo © *Fernando Cordero*
p. 145

The Westin Resort & Spa, 1989
Los Cabos San Lucas,
BCS, Mexico
Photo © *Fernando Cordero*
p. 150

Casa de Los Magueyes, 1996
Mexico City, Mexico
Photo © *Undine Prohl*
p. 152

Casa Celosía, 2006
Cancún, Quintana Roo, Mexico
Photo © *Michael Calderwood*
p. 157

Casa de Los Magueyes, 1996
Mexico City, Mexico
Photo © *Alfonso de Béjar*
p. 158

Rancho Huracán, 1989
Nayarit, Mexico
Photo © *Fernando Cordero*
p. 165

Caballeriza Los Manantiales, 2008
Valle de Bravo,
State of Mexico, Mexico
Photo © *Michael Calderwood*
p. 171

Rancho Huracán, 1989
Nayarit, Mexico
Photo © *Fernando Cordero*
p. 178

Casa de Los Magueyes, 1996
Mexico City, Mexico
Photo © *Fernando Cordero*
p. 159

Rancho Huracán, 1989
Nayarit, Mexico
Photo © *Fernando Cordero*
p. 166

Caballeriza Los Manantiales, 2008
Valle de Bravo,
State of Mexico, Mexico
Photo © *Michael Calderwood*
p. 172

Rancho Huracán, 1989
Nayarit, Mexico
Photo © *Fernando Cordero*
p. 179

Casa Las Palmas 1, 2002
Punta Mita, Nayarit, Mexico
Photo © *Fernando Cordero*
pp. 160, 161

Rancho Huracán, 1989
Nayarit, Mexico
Photo © *Fernando Cordero*
p. 167

Caballeriza Los Manantiales, 2008
Valle de Bravo,
State of Mexico, Mexico
Photo © *Michael Calderwood*
p. 173

Costa Baja Resort & Marina, 2004
BCS, La Paz, Mexico
Photo © *Michael Calderwood*
p. 180

Rancho Huracán, 1989
Nayarit, Mexico
Photo © *Fernando Cordero*
pp. 162, 163

Conjunto Izar 2, 1999
Valle de Bravo,
State of Mexico, Mexico
Photo © *Fernando Cordero*
pp. 168, 169

Caballeriza Los Manantiales, 2008
Valle de Bravo,
State of Mexico, Mexico
Photo © *Michael Calderwood*
pp. 174, 175

Costa Baja Resort & Marina, 2004
BCS, La Paz, México
Photo © *Michael Calderwood*
p. 181

Rancho Huracán, 1989
Nayarit, Mexico
Photo © *Fernando Cordero*
p. 164

Caballeriza Los Manantiales, 2008
Valle de Bravo,
State of Mexico, Mexico
Photo © *Michael Calderwood*
p. 170

Caballeriza Los Manantiales, 2008
Valle de Bravo,
State of Mexico, Mexico
Photo © *Michael Calderwood*
p. 177

Costa Baja Resort & Marina, 2004
BCS, La Paz, Mexico
Photo © *Michael Calderwood*
p. 182

Costa Baja Resort & Marina, 2004
BCS, La Paz, Mexico
Photo © *Michael Calderwood*
p. 183

Casa Las Palmas 1, 2002
Punta Mita, Nayarit, Mexico
Photo © *Fernando Cordero*
p. 189

The Westin Resort & Spa, 1989
Los Cabos, BCS, Mexico
Photo © *Fernando Cordero*
p. 195

Caballerizas Hacienda Santa Rosa, 2008
Valle de Bravo,
State of Mexico, Mexico
Photo © *Michael Calderwood*
p. 201

Casa Celosía, 2006
Cancún, Quintana Roo, Mexico
Photo © *Michael Calderwood*
pp. 184, 185

Casa Las Palmas 1, 2002
Punta Mita, Nayarit, Mexico
Photo © *Fernando Cordero*
pp. 190, 191

Casa Las Palapas, 1996
Nayarit, Mexico
Photo © *Arturo Zavala Haag*
p. 196

Caballerizas Hacienda Santa Rosa, 2008
Valle de Bravo,
State of Mexico, Mexico
Photo © *Michael Calderwood*
p. 202

Casa Celosía, 2006
Cancún, Quintana Roo, Mexico
Photo © *Michael Calderwood*
p. 186

Casa de Las Palmas 1, 2002
Punta Mita, Nayarit, Mexico
Photo © *Miguel García*
p. 192

Casa Las Palapas, 1996
Nayarit, Mexico
Photo © *Arturo Zavala Haag*
p. 197

Caballerizas Hacienda Santa Rosa, 2008
Valle de Bravo,
State of Mexico, Mexico
Photo © *Michael Calderwood*
p. 203

Casa Celosía, 2006
Cancún, Quintana Roo, Mexico
Photo © *Michael Calderwood*
p. 187

Casa Las Palmas 1, 2002
Punta Mita, Nayarit, Mexico
Photo © *Fernando Cordero*
p. 193

Caballerizas Hacienda Santa Rosa, 2008
Valle de Bravo,
State of Mexico, Mexico
Photo © *Michael Calderwood*
pp. 198, 199

Casona Chimalistac, 1981
Condumex, Mexico City, Mexico
Photo © *Mario Mutschlechner*
p. 204

Casa Las Palmas 1, 2002
Punta Mita, Nayarit, Mexico
Photo © *Fernando Cordero*
p. 188

Casa Las Palmas 1, 2002
Punta Mita, Nayarit, Mexico
Photo © *Fernando Cordero*
p. 194

Caballerizas Hacienda Santa Rosa, 2008
Valle de Bravo,
State of Mexico, Mexico
Photo © *Michael Calderwood*
p. 200

Casona Chimalistac, 1981
Condumex, Mexico City, Mexico
Photo © *Mario Mutschlechner*
p. 205

The Westin Resort Spa, 1989-1992
Pto. Vallarta, Jalisco, Mexico
Photo © *Paul Czitrom*
p. 206

Torre Alta, 1982
Monterrey, Nuevo León,
Mexico
Photo © *Arturo Zavala Haag*
p. 209

Rancho Huracán, 1994
Nayarit, Mexico
Photo © *Fernando Cordero*
p. 212

Hegel, 2004
Mexico City, Mexico
Photo © *Michael Calderwood*
p. 215

The Westin Resort Spa, 1989-1992
Pto. Vallarta, Jalisco, Mexico
Photo © *Paul Czitrom*
p. 207

Banco Santander Serfin, 1994
Mexico City, Mexico
Photo © *Fernando Cordero*
p. 210

Casa Las Palmas 1, 2002
Punta Mita, Nayarit, Mexico
Photo © *Fernando Cordero*
p. 213

Luz Saviñón, 2004
Mexico City, Mexico
Photo © *Michael Calderwood*
pp. 216, 217

Torre Alta, 1982
Monterrey, Nuevo León,
Mexico
Photo © *Arturo Zavala Haag*
p. 208

Banco Santander Serfin, 1994
Mexico City, Mexico
Photo © *Fernando Cordero*
p. 211

Luz Saviñón, 2004
Mexico City, Mexico
Photo © *Michael Calderwood*
p. 214

*José de Yturbe, Andrés Cajiga
Ramírez, José de Yturbe Sordo*
Mexico City, Mexico, 2005
Photo © *Graciela Iturbide*
p. 222

Torre Alta, 1982
Monterrey, Nuevo León,
Mexico
Photo © *Arturo Zavala Haag*
p. 209

Banco Santander Serfin, 1994
Mexico City, Mexico
Photo © *Fernando Cordero*
p. 211

Hegel, 2004
Mexico City, Mexico
Photo © *Michael Calderwood*
p. 215

Torre Alta, 1982
Monterrey, Nuevo León,
Mexico
Photo © *Arturo Zavala Haag*
p. 209

Banco Santander Serfin, 1994
Mexico City, Mexico
Photo © *Fernando Cordero*
p. 211

Hegel, 2004
Mexico City, Mexico
Photo © *Michael Calderwood*
p. 215

ICONS **DE YTURBE** ARQUITECTOS

was printed and bound in June 2008 in the presses of EBS Editoriale Bortolazzi in Verona, Italy. Types of the Futura and Lino Type Didot Roman LH and OF family were used. It was printed on 150-gram Estucado arte paper. The printing was supervised and overseen by Jimena Gutiérrez and Ricardo Salas.